METALLICA:
CLASSIC SONGS
NOTE-FOR-NOTE TRANSCRIPTIONS WITH DVD

Cherry Lane Music Company
Director of Publications/Project Editor: Mark Phillips
Project Coordinator: Rebecca Skidmore

ISBN 978-1-60378-321-7

Visit our website at www.cherrylaneprint.com

CONTENTS

HIT THE LIGHTS

Words and Music by
James Hetfield and Lars Ulrich

1. No life till leath - er. ___ We're gon - na kick some ass ___ to - night.
2.3. *See additional lyrics*

Got the met - al mad - ness. When our fans start scream - in' it's right. Well al -

right, ___ yeah. ___ When we start to rock ___ we

nev - er ___ will stop a - gain. ___ Hit the ___

lights. Hit the ___ lights. ___

Fill 1 (end of Interlude I)

Fill 2 (end of Interlude II)

Additional Lyrics

2. Know our fans are insane.
   We're gonna blow this place away
   With volume higher
   Than anything today. The only way.
   When we start to rock we never, *etc.*

3. With all out screamin'
   We're gonna rip right through your brain.
   We got the lethal power.
   It's causin' you sweet pain. Oh sweet pain.
   When we start to rock we never, *etc.*

FOR WHOM THE BELL TOLLS

Words and Music by
James Hetfield, Lars Ulrich
and Cliff Burton

1st, 2nd Verses
w/Rhy. Fig. 2 (2 times)

1. Make his fight on the hill in the ear-ly day. Con-stant chill deep in-
2. Take a look to the sky just be-fore you die. It's the last time he

side. Shout-ing gun, on they run through the end-less grey.
will. Black-ened roar, mas-sive roar fills the crum-bling sky.

On they fight, for they're right.__ Yes, but who's to say? For a hill men would
Shat-tered goal fills his soul__ with a ruth-less cry. Stran-ger now are his

kill. Why? They do not know. Suf-ferred wounds test their pride.
eyes to this mys-ter-y. Hears the si-lence so loud.

Men of five, still a-live__ through the rag-ing glow. Gone in-sane from the pain__
Crack of dawn, all is gone ex-cept the will to be. Now they see what will be,__

Chorus
w/Rhy. Fig. 3 (2 times)

__ that they sure-ly know..}
__ blind-ed eyes to see.__}

For whom the bell__ tolls.__

Time march-es on for whom the bell__ tolls._____

LEPER MESSIAH

Words and Music by
James Hetfield and Lars Ulrich

14

Bridge
w/Rhy. Fig. 2

Witch - er - y,___ weak - en - ing,___ sees the sheep___ are gath - er - ing.___

Set the trap,___ hyp - no - tize.___ Now you fol - low.

Guitar solo

Rhy.
Fig. 3

w/Rhy. Fig. 3

...AND JUSTICE FOR ALL

Words and Music by
James Hetfield, Lars Ulrich
and Kirk Hammett

1st, 2nd, 3rd Verses

w/Rhy. Fig. 2 *(2 times)*

1. Halls of jus - tice paint - ed green. Mon - ey talk - ing.___
2. Ap - a - thy their step - ping - stone. So un - feel - ing.___
3. La - dy jus - tice has been raped. Truth as - sas - sin.___

Pow - er wolves be - set your door, hear them stalk - ing.
Hid - den deep an - i - mos - i - ty, so de - ceiv - ing.
Rolls of red tape seal your lips. Now your done in.

Soon you'll please their ap - pe - tite, they de - vour.___
Through your eyes their light burns, hop - ing to find.___
Their mon - ey tips her scales a - gain. Make your deal.___

Ham - mer of jus - tice crush - es you. O - ver - pow - er.__
In - qui - si - tion seek - ing you with cry - ing __ might.__
Just what is truth? I can - not tell, can - not feel.__

The ul - ti - mate in van - i - ty.__

Ex - ploit - ing their __ su - prem -

Rhy. Fill 1

Rhy. Fill 2

*Vocal rests for two bars.

25

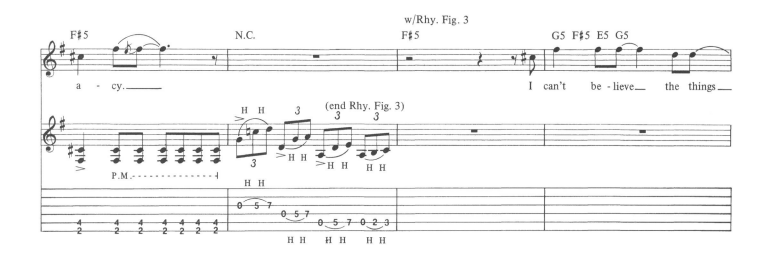

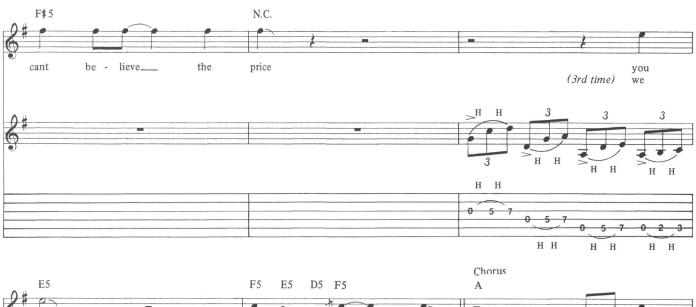

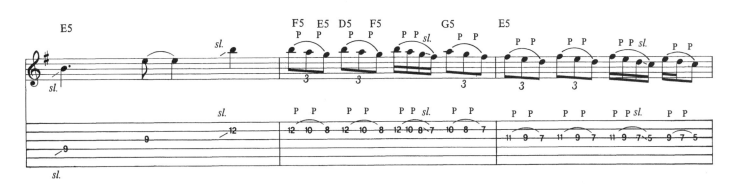

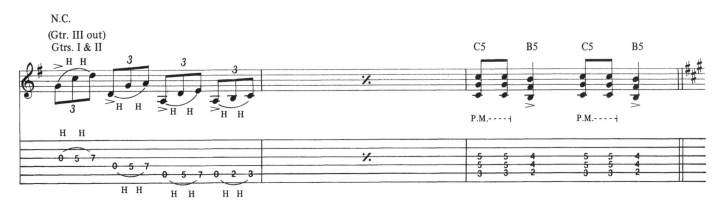

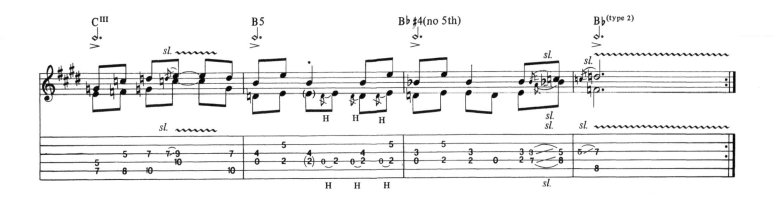

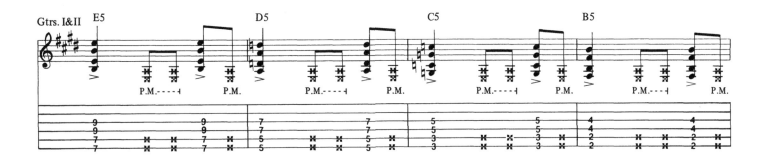

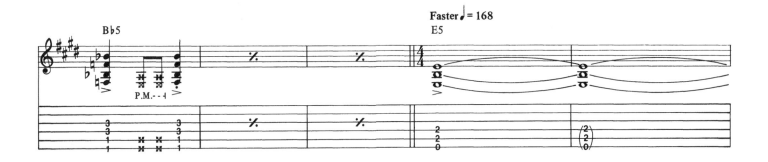

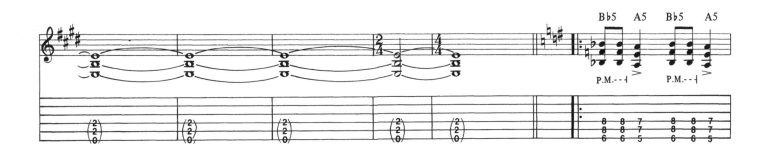

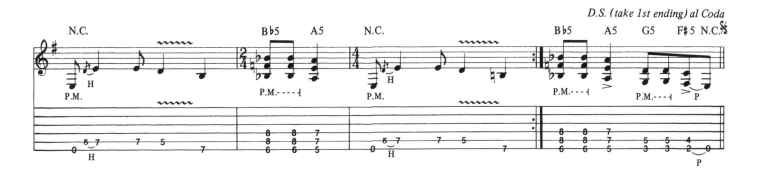

WHEREVER I MAY ROAM

Words and Music by
James Hetfield and Lars Ulrich

E5 N.C. E5 N.C.
both gtrs. Gtr. II both gtrs. Gtr. II
P.M. Gtr. III
*P.M. Gtr. III
*P.M. refers to both gtrs.
Pre-chorus
w/Rhy. Fig. 4
F5 N.C. E5
But I'll take my time an - y - where. I'm free to
N.C. Bb5 N.C.
speak my mind. And I'll take my find an - y - where.
Half time feel
Chorus
A5
An - y - where I roam,
G5
(end half time feel)
where I lay my head is home, that's where.
Guitar solo
w/Rhy. Fig. 1 (2 times)
Gtr. V
E5 N.C.
(w/wah)
sl.
1/2
Full
E5 N.C. A5 A#5 B5 C5 E5 N.C.
8va
*Tap w/edge of pick.
8va
E5 N.C.
loco

41

Additional Lyrics

2. And the earth becomes my throne,
   I adapt to the unknown.
   Under wandering stars I've grown,
   By myself but not alone.
   I ask no one.
   And my ties are severed clean,
   The less I have, the more I gain.
   Off the beaten path I reign.
   Rover, wanderer, nomad, vagabond,
   Call me what you will. *(To Pre-chorus)*

UNTIL IT SLEEPS

Words and Music by
James Hetfield and Lars Ulrich

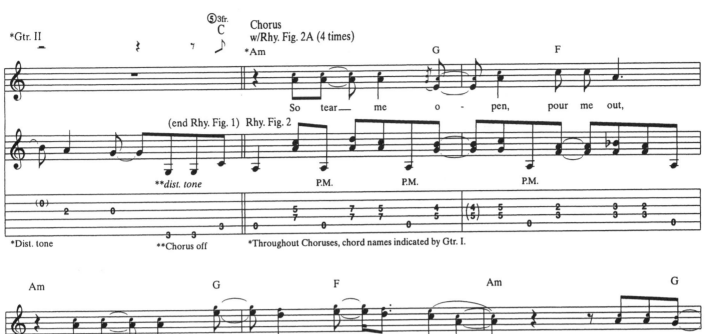

So tear— me o - pen, pour me out,

there's things— in - side— that scream— and shout.— And the pain—

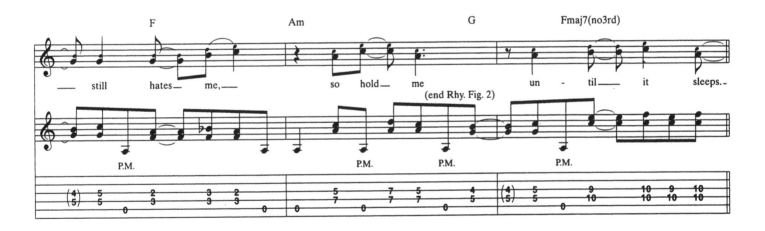

— still hates— me,— so hold— me un - til— it sleeps..

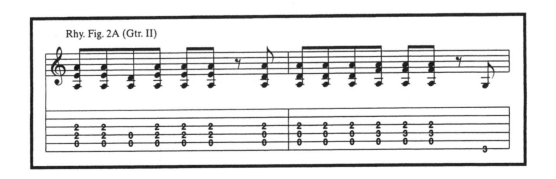

Rhy. Fig. 2A (Gtr. II)

A5   G   Fsus2

dim.

Gtr. II

clean tone w/chorus

let ring

Rhy. Fig. 3 (Gtr. I)   (end Rhy. Fig. 3)

clean tone w/chorus
let ring

2nd Verse
w/Rhy. Fig. 1
*Am   N.C.

Just   like——   the   curse,——   just   like the   stray.——

Gtr. II

let ring

*Throughout Verses, chord names indicated by Gtr. I.

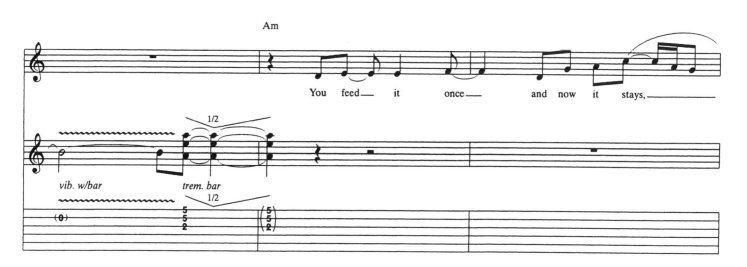

Am

You feed—— it   once——   and now it   stays,——

vib. w/bar   1/2
trem. bar
1/2

48

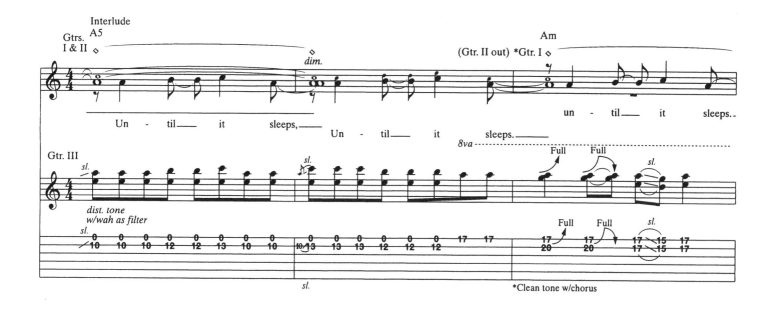

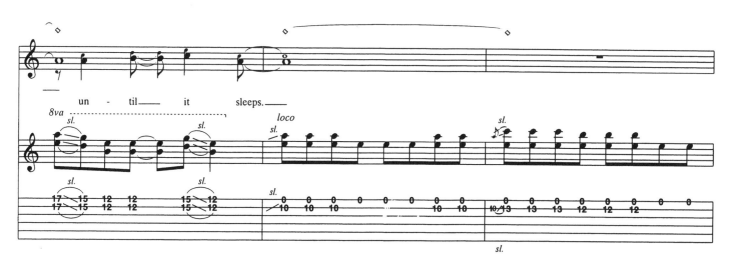

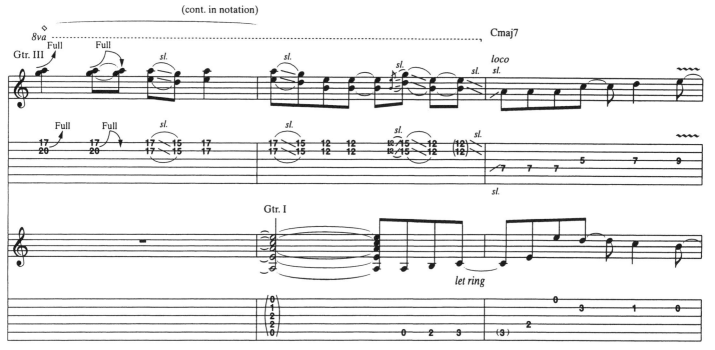

Don't want___ it.___

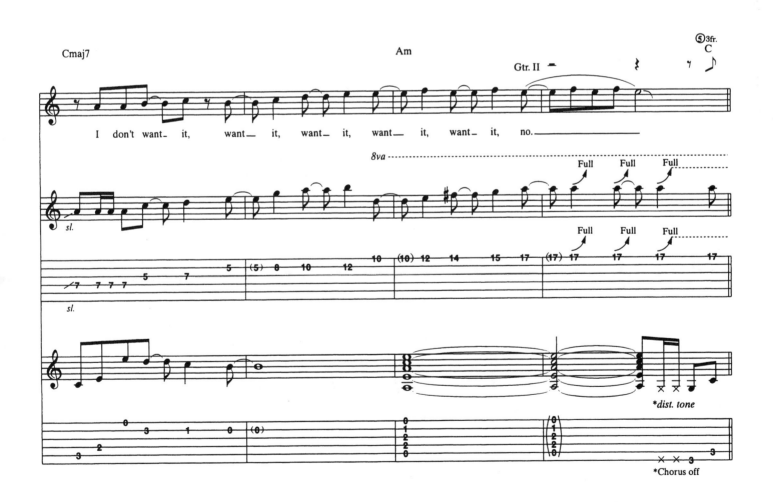

I don't want___ it, want___ it, want___ it, want___ it, want___ it, no.___

*dist. tone

*Chorus off

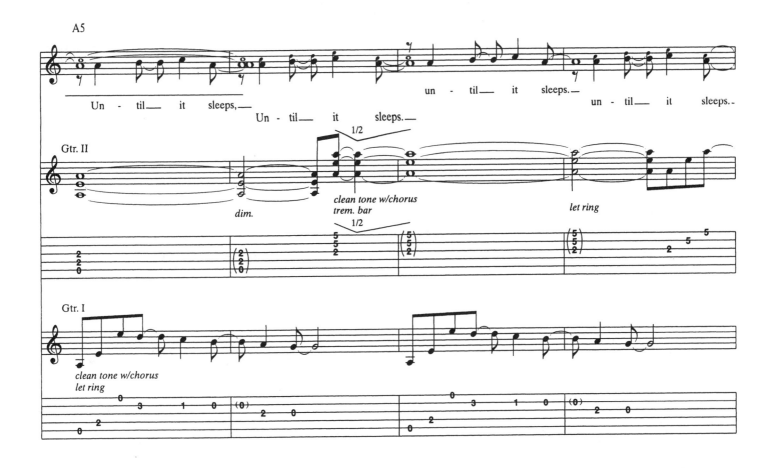

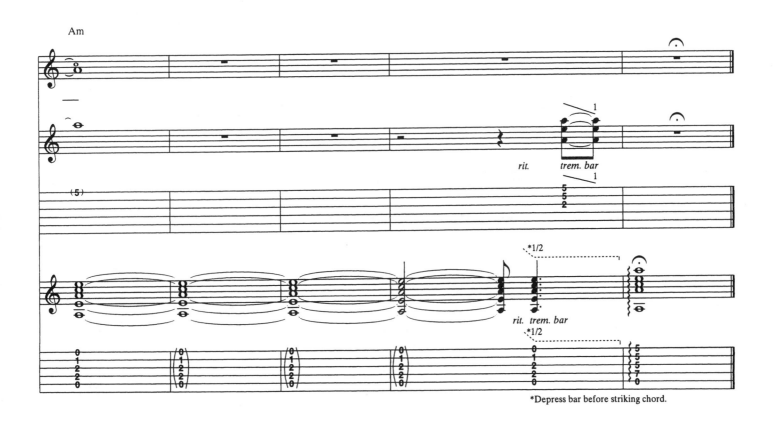

*Depress bar before striking chord.

THE MEMORY REMAINS

Words and Music by
James Hetfield and Lars Ulrich

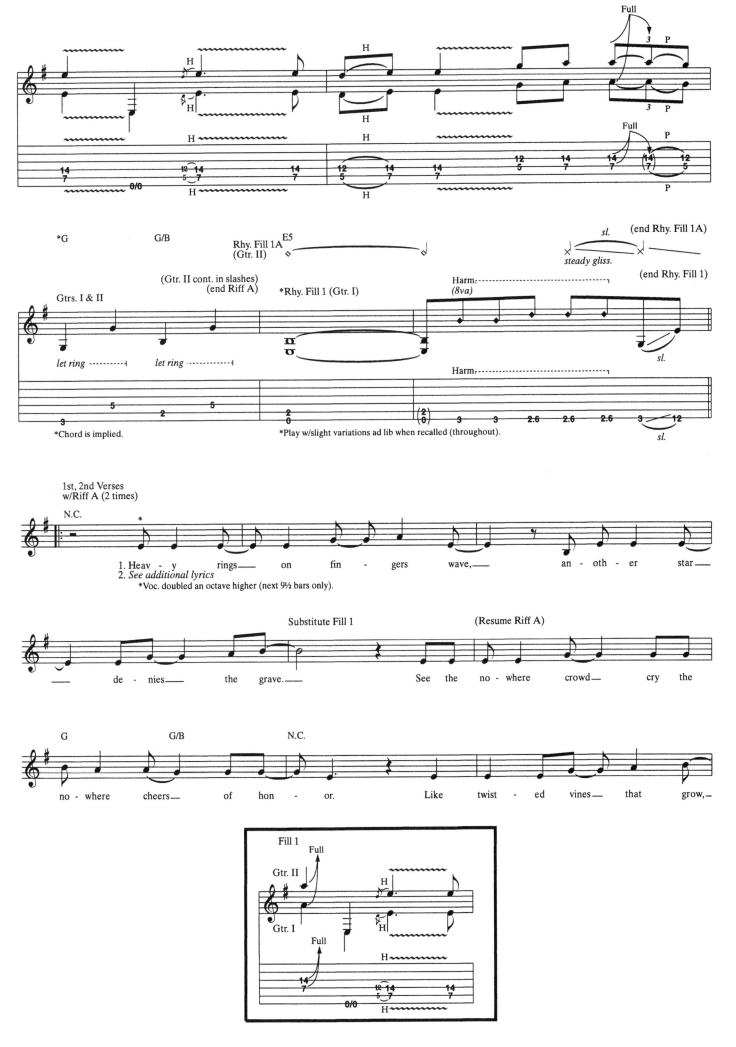

1st time substitute Fill 2 (Gtrs. I&II)
2nd time substitute Fills 2 (Gtr. II) & 2A (Gtr. I)
(Resume Riff A)
hide and swal - low man - sions whole, and dim the light
1st time w/Rhy. Fills 1 & 1A
2nd time w/Rhy. Fills *1A & 1B
G G/B E5
of an al - read - y fad - ed pri - ma don - na.
*Let E5 chord ring through entire 2nd bar; omit slide.
Chorus
D5 E5 N.C. E5
For - tune, fame, mir - ror vain, gone in - sane...
Rhy. Fig. 1 (Gtrs. I & II)
(end Rhy. Fig. 1)
P.M.
Fill 2
Gtr. II
Gtr. I
Full
H
Fill 2A (Gtr. I)
Full
H
Rhy. Fill 1B (Gtr. I)
sl.

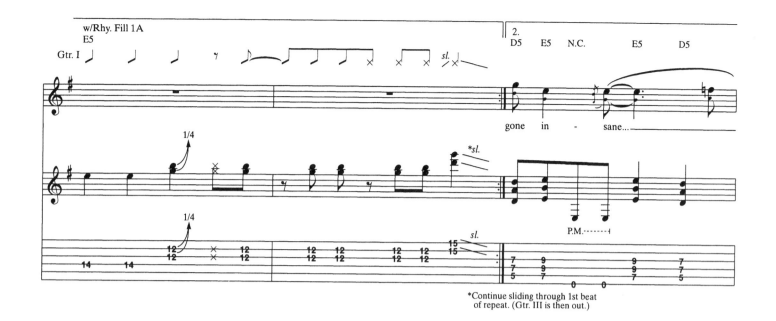

*Continue sliding through 1st beat
of repeat. (Gtr. III is then out.)

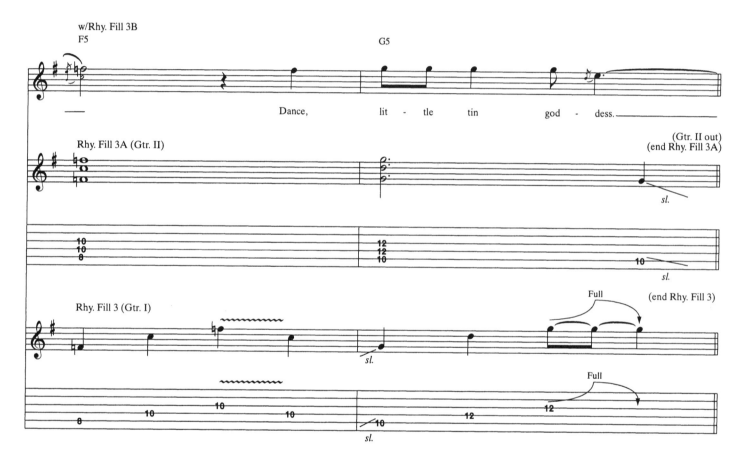

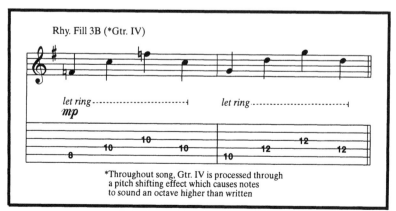

*Throughout song, Gtr. IV is processed through
a pitch shifting effect which causes notes
to sound an octave higher than written

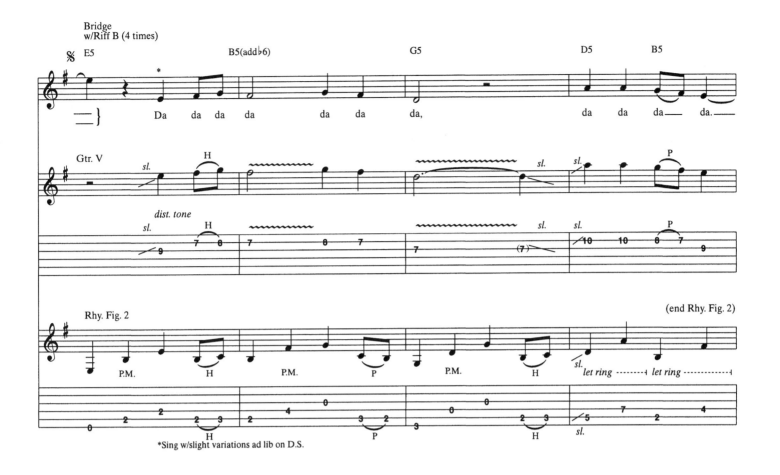

*Sing w/slight variations ad lib on D.S.

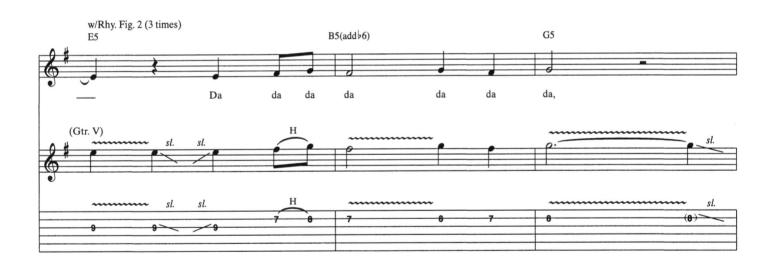

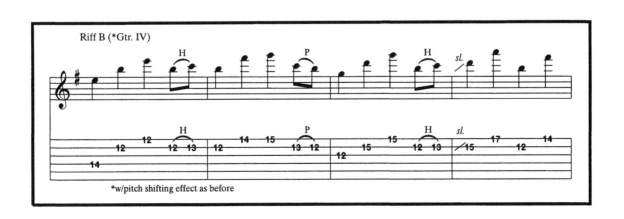

*w/pitch shifting effect as before

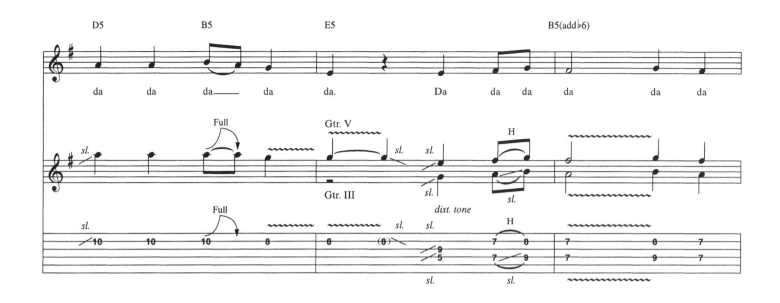

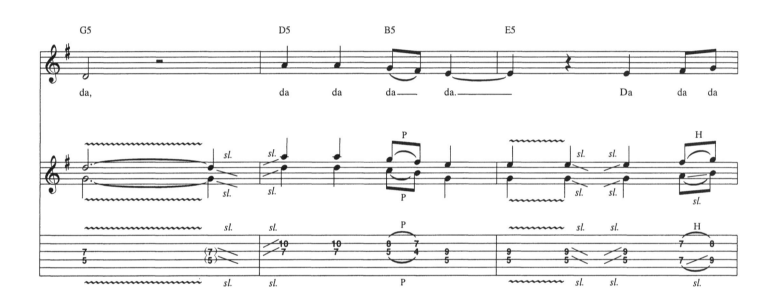

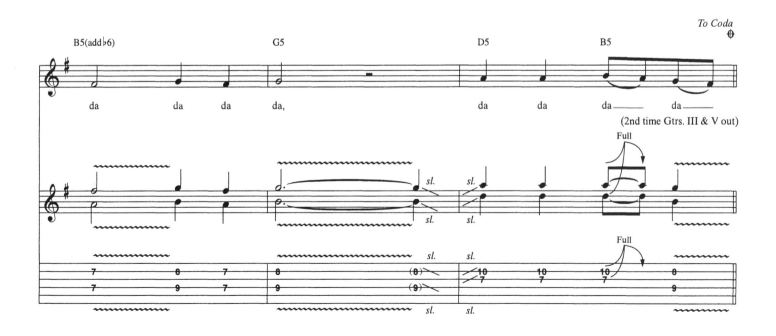

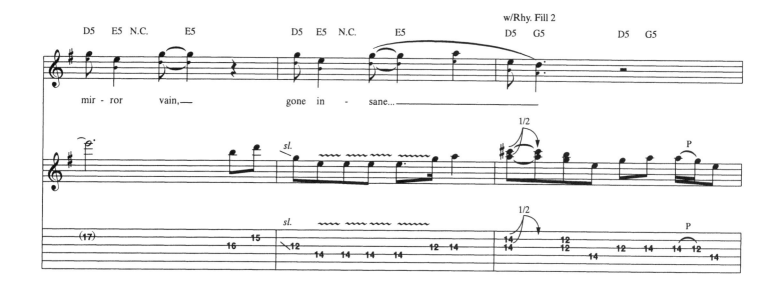

mir - ror vain,___ gone in - sane...___

For - tune, fame,___ mir - ror vain,___ gone in - sane,___ but the

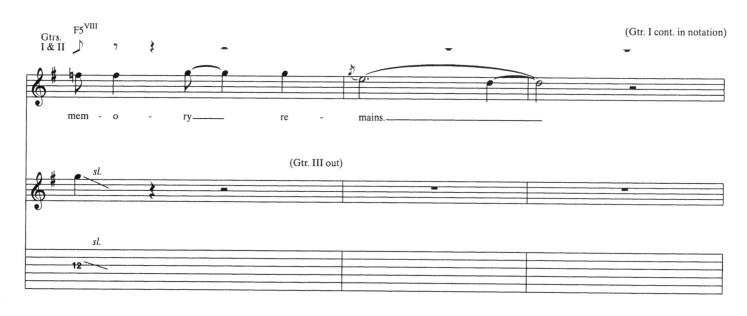

mem - o - ry___ re - mains.___

(Gtr. III out)

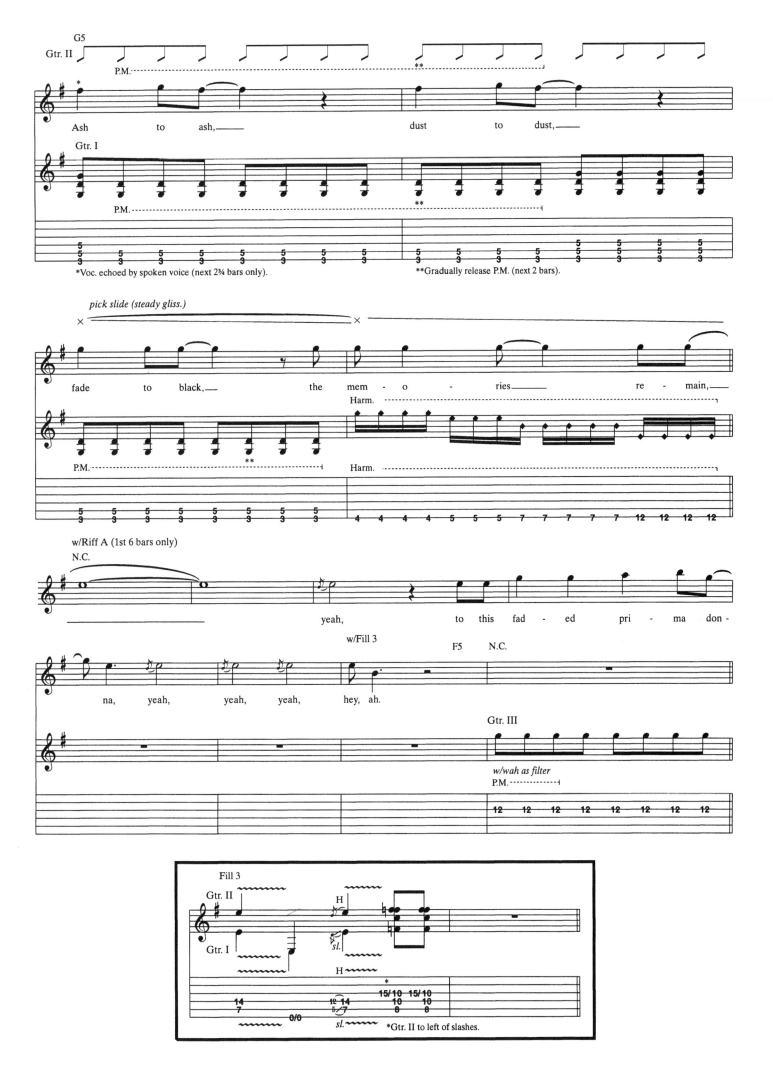

Guitar solo
w/Riff A (1st 3 bars only)
N.C.

w/Fill 4

D5　　E5

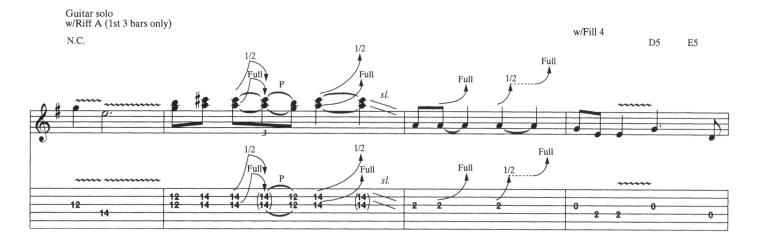

w/Riff A (1st 3 bars only)
N.C.

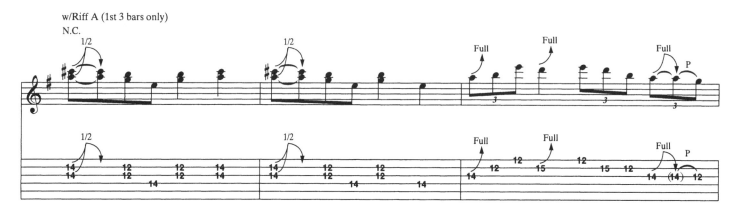

w/Rhy. Fills 3, 3A & 3B
F5

G5

D.S. al Coda
%

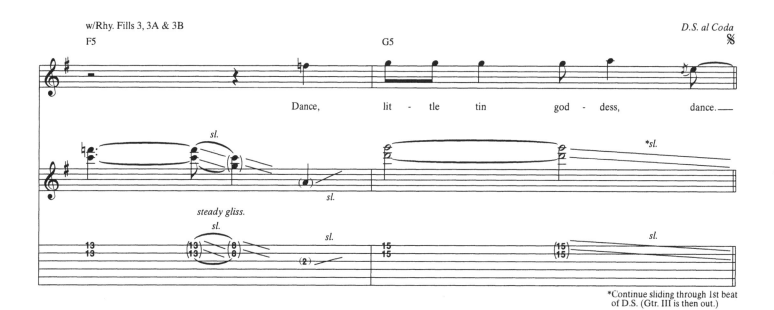

Dance, lit - tle tin god - dess, dance.___

*Continue sliding through 1st beat
of D.S. (Gtr. III is then out.)

*Gtr. IV gradually fades out, substituting Fill 5 for 4th bar of Riff B,
2nd and 4th times only. Gtr. IV continues playing in 4/4 regardless of vocal
singing in 2/4 for one bar.

*w/pitch shifting effect as before

Additional Lyrics

2. Heavy rings hold cigarettes
   Up to lips that time forgets
   While the Hollywood sun sets
   Behind your back.
   And can't the band play on?
   Just listen, they play my song.
   Ash to ash, dust to dust,
   Fade to black. *(To Chorus)*

FRANTIC

Words and Music by
James Hetfield, Lars Ulrich,
Kirk Hammett and Bob Rock

Drop D tuning, down 1 step:
(low to high) C-G-C-F-A-D

Intro

Moderately fast Rock ♩ = 168

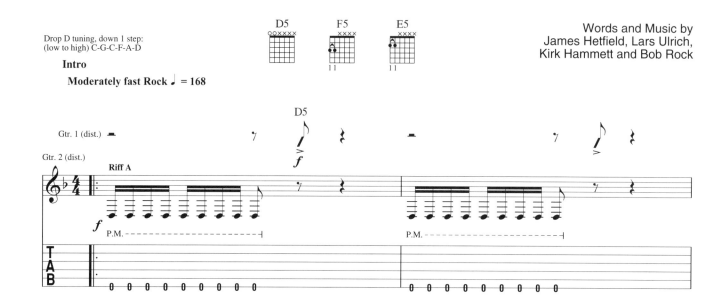

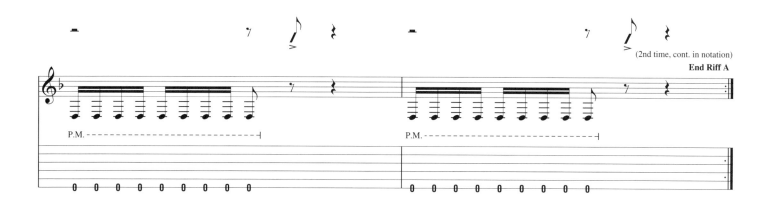

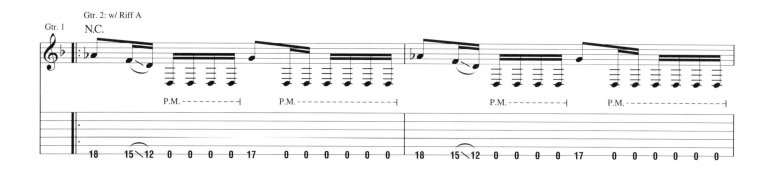

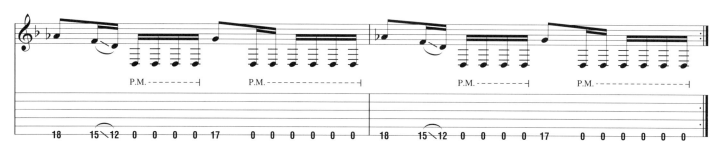

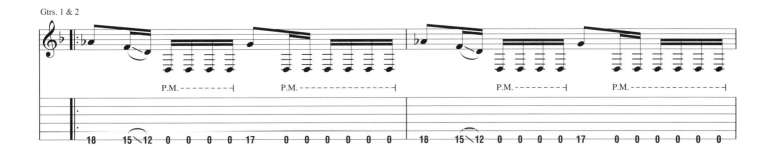

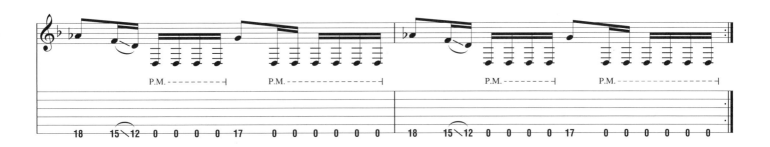

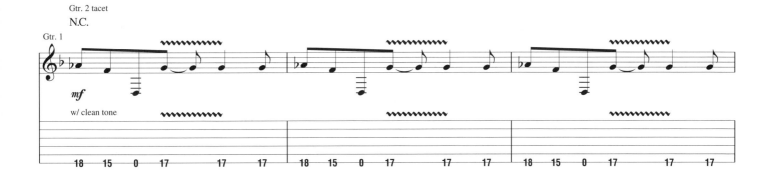

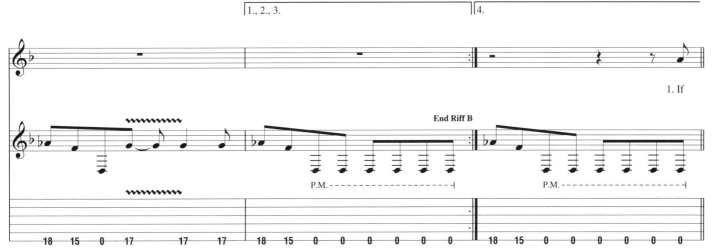

Verse

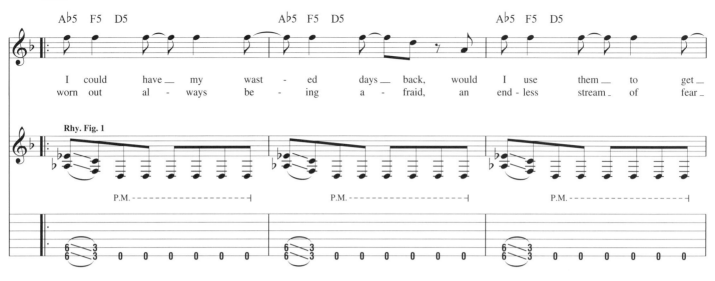

I could have __ my wast - ed days back, would I use them __ to get __
worn out al - ways be - ing a - fraid, an end - less stream __ of fear __

Rhy. Fig. 1

P.M.

Gtr. 1: w/ Rhy. Fig. 1 (1st 3 meas.)
Gtr. 2: w/ Rhy. Fig. 1

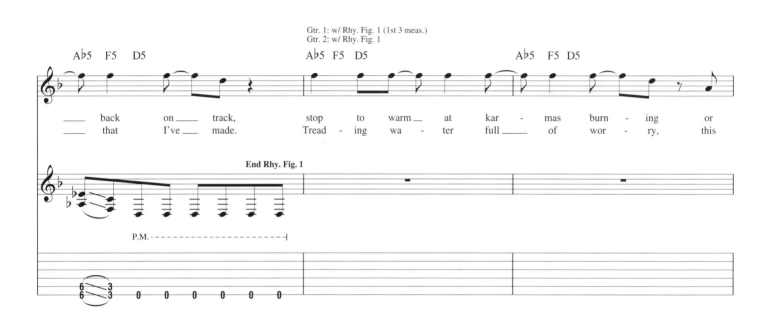

__ back on __ track, stop to warm __ at kar - mas burn - ing or
__ that I've __ made. Tread - ing wa - ter full __ of wor - ry, this

End Rhy. Fig. 1

P.M.

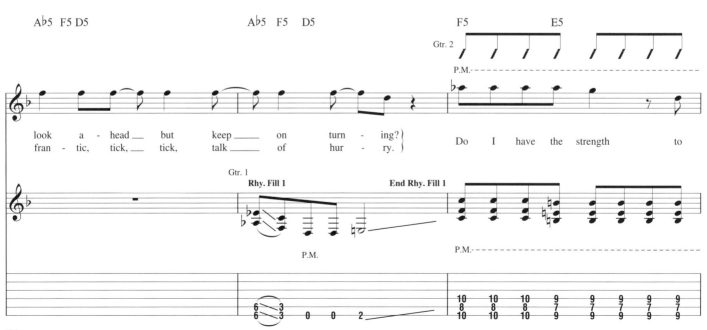

look a - head __ but keep __ on turn - ing?⎫ Do I have the strength to
fran - tic, tick, __ tick, talk __ of hur - ry.⎭

Gtr. 1
Rhy. Fill 1

Gtr. 2

P.M.

End Rhy. Fill 1

P.M.

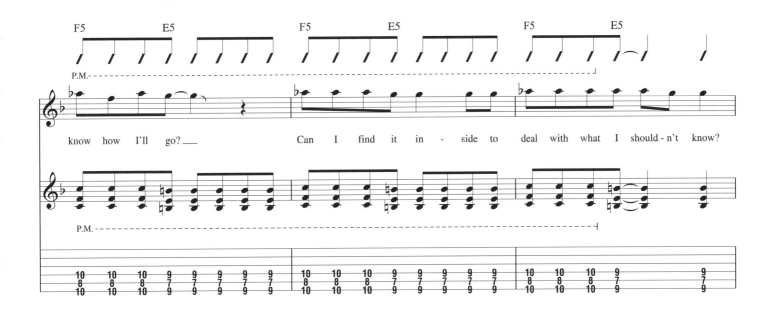

know how I'll go? ___ Can I find it in - side to deal with what I should - n't know?

End half-time feel

Gtr. 1: w/ Rhy. Fig. 1 (1st 3 meas.)
Gtr. 2: w/ Rhy. Fig. 1

Gtr. 1: w/ Rhy. Fill 1

A♭5 F5 D5   A♭5 F5 D5   A♭5 F5 D5   A♭5 F5 D5

{ Could I have ___ my wast - ed days ___ back? Would I use them ___ to get ___ back on ___ track? }
{ Worn out al - ways be - ing a - fraid, an end - less stream ___ of fear ___ that I've ___ made. }

N.C.

You live it or lie ___ it! You

Gtr. 1   Gtrs. 1 & 2

mf   *f*
w/ clean tone   w/ dist.

Gtr. 2 tacet

live it or lie ___ it!   (You live it or lie ___ it! You live it or lie ___ it!   My

Gtr. 1

mf
w/ clean tone

life - style   de - ter - mines my death - style.   My life - style   de - ter - mines my death - style.

𝄋 Pre-Chorus
Half-time feel

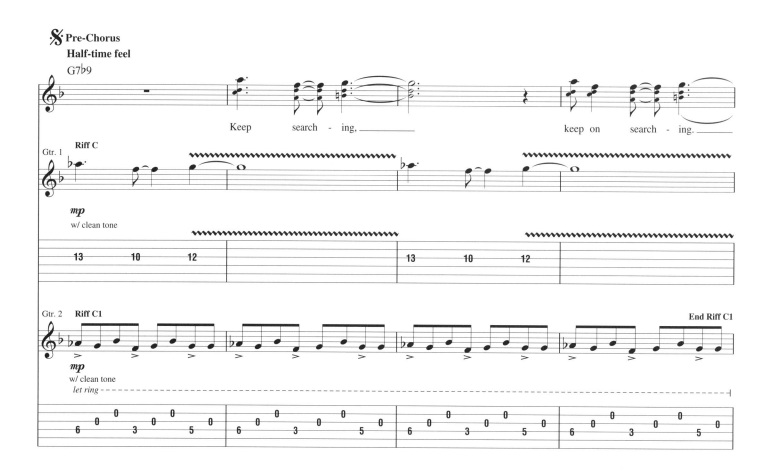

Keep   search - ing, _____   keep on   search - ing. _____

Gtr. 2: w/ Riff C1 (3 times)

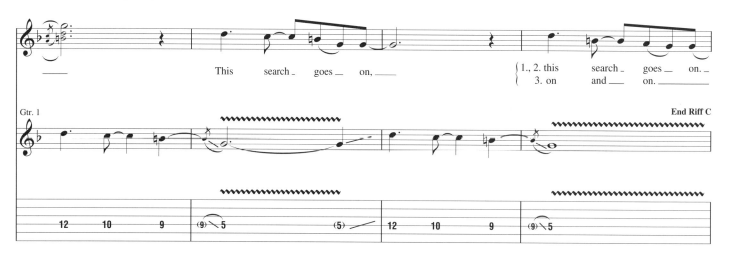

This   search __ goes __ on, _____   { 1., 2. this   search __ goes __ on. __
{ 3. on   and ___ on. ___

Gtr. 1: w/ Riff C

Keep   search - ing, _____   keep on   search - ing.

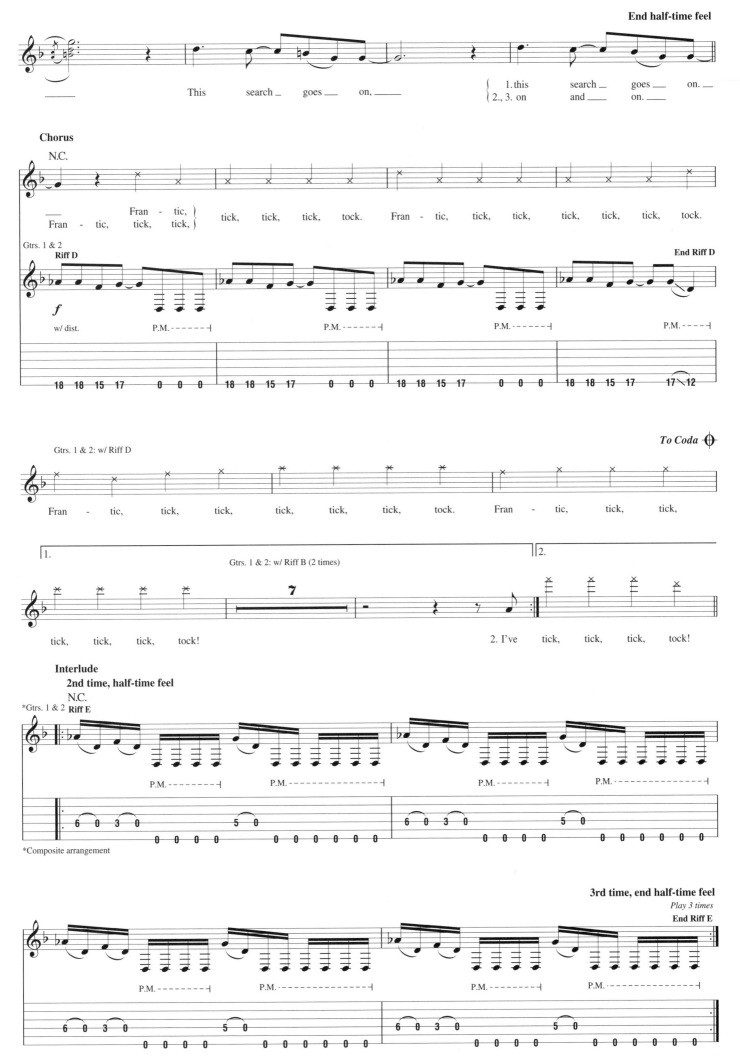

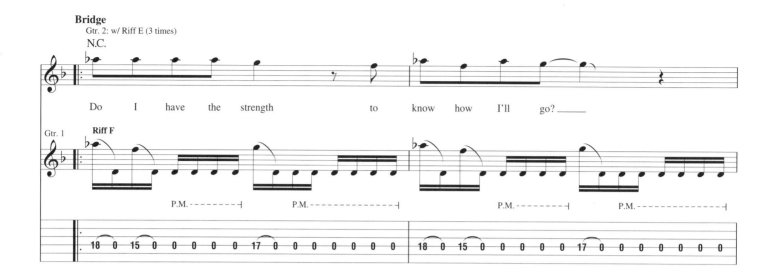

Bridge
Gtr. 2: w/ Riff E (3 times)

N.C.

Do I have the strength to know how I'll go? _____

Gtr. 1 — **Riff F**

P.M. -------- ⌐   P.M. -------------- ⌐   P.M. -------- ⌐   P.M. ------------ ⌐

Can I find it in - side to deal with what I should - n't know? _____

End Riff F

P.M. -------- ⌐   P.M. -------------- ⌐   P.M. -------- ⌐   P.M. ------------ ⌐

|1.
Gtr. 1: w/ Riff F

|2.
Gtr. 1: w/ Riff E
Gtr. 2: w/ Riff A

_____   _____   Oh. _____ My

Gtr. 2: w/ Riff A (2 times)

D5

life - style   (Birth is pain.)   de - ter - mines my death - style,   a

Gtr. 1 — **Riff G**

P.M. ------------------- ⌐   P.M. ------------------- ⌐

GUITAR NOTATION LEGEND

Guitar music can be notated three different ways: on a *musical staff*, in *tablature*, and in *rhythm slashes*.

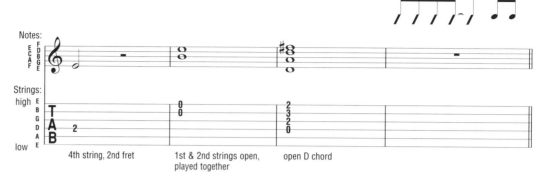

RHYTHM SLASHES are written above the staff. Strum chords in the rhythm indicated. Use the chord diagrams found at the top of the first page of the transcription for the appropriate chord voicings. Round noteheads indicate single notes.

THE MUSICAL STAFF shows pitches and rhythms and is divided by bar lines into measures. Pitches are named after the first seven letters of the alphabet.

TABLATURE graphically represents the guitar fingerboard. Each horizontal line represents a string, and each number represents a fret.

4th string, 2nd fret   1st & 2nd strings open, played together   open D chord

---

HALF-STEP BEND: Strike the note and bend up 1/2 step.

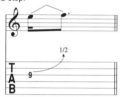

WHOLE-STEP BEND: Strike the note and bend up one step.

GRACE NOTE BEND: Strike the note and immediately bend up as indicated.

SLIGHT (MICROTONE) BEND: Strike the note and bend up 1/4 step.

BEND AND RELEASE: Strike the note and bend up as indicated, then release back to the original note. Only the first note is struck.

PRE-BEND: Bend the note as indicated, then strike it.

VIBRATO: The string is vibrated by rapidly bending and releasing the note with the fretting hand.

WIDE VIBRATO: The pitch is varied to a greater degree by vibrating with the fretting hand.

HAMMER-ON: Strike the first (lower) note with one finger, then sound the higher note (on the same string) with another finger by fretting it without picking.

PULL-OFF: Place both fingers on the notes to be sounded. Strike the first note and without picking, pull the finger off to sound the second (lower) note.

LEGATO SLIDE: Strike the first note and then slide the same fret-hand finger up or down to the second note. The second note is not struck.

SHIFT SLIDE: Same as legato slide, except the second note is struck.

TRILL: Very rapidly alternate between the notes indicated by continuously hammering on and pulling off.

TAPPING: Hammer ("tap") the fret indicated with the pick-hand index or middle finger and pull off to the note fretted by the fret hand.

NATURAL HARMONIC: Strike the note while the fret-hand lightly touches the string directly over the fret indicated.

PINCH HARMONIC: The note is fretted normally and a harmonic is produced by adding the edge of the thumb or the tip of the index finger of the pick hand to the normal pick attack.

PICK SCRAPE: The edge of the pick is rubbed down (or up) the string, producing a scratchy sound.

MUFFLED STRINGS: A percussive sound is produced by laying the fret hand across the string(s) without depressing, and striking them with the pick hand.

PALM MUTING: The note is partially muted by the pick hand lightly touching the string(s) just before the bridge.

RAKE: Drag the pick across the strings indicated with a single motion.

TREMOLO PICKING: The note is picked as rapidly and continuously as possible.

VIBRATO BAR DIVE AND RETURN: The pitch of the note or chord is dropped a specified number of steps (in rhythm), then returned to the original pitch.

VIBRATO BAR SCOOP: Depress the bar just before striking the note, then quickly release the bar.

VIBRATO BAR DIP: Strike the note and then immediately drop a specified number of steps, then release back to the original pitch.